Original title:
The Ice Hour

Copyright © 2024 Swan Charm
All rights reserved.

Author: Paulina Pähkel
ISBN HARDBACK: 978-9916-79-927-7
ISBN PAPERBACK: 978-9916-79-928-4
ISBN EBOOK: 978-9916-79-929-1

Icicle Monologue

In the quiet of winter's breath,
Icicles hang like whispers of death.
They glisten bright in the pale light,
Silent watchers of the dark night.

Dripping slowly, a melody unheard,
A symphony played by the frozen bird.
Each drop echoes a moment spent,
Time's slow passage in pure lament.

They twist and turn, in shapes divine,
Nature's art from ice and brine.
Fragile beauty, soon to depart,
A fleeting glimpse of the winter's heart.

As the sun rises, they start to weep,
Liquid pearls from secrets they keep.
Emotions thaw in the warming ray,
Echoes of thoughts from yesterday.

So I speak to these frozen forms,
Conversations born in winter storms.
Their silence echoes my own refrain,
In the chill, we share the pain.

Frosted Lore

Beneath the frost, old stories lie,
Whispers of tales where memories die.
Each layer thick with history's voice,
A tapestry woven, devoid of choice.

The frosted leaves speak of love's loss,
Each breath a chill, a heavy cost.
Nature's script on a canvas white,
Illuminates dreams that fade from sight.

In the heart of the woods, shadows convene,
Echoing secrets of what once had been.
The chill wraps tight, a spectral cloak,
Every rustle a word, each silence a joke.

Unraveled stories in the drifting snow,
Footprints tell where the lost hearts go.
With every step, the legends grow,
In luminescent frost, time's steady flow.

So listen close to the frosted lore,
In every whisper, a tale to explore.
Embrace the cold where the stories lie,
For beneath the frost, old dreams never die.

Glare of the Pale Sun

In the morning, the pale sun appears,
Casting shadows and softening fears.
The world awakens with a tender glow,
Each ray a promise, a gentle flow.

Snowflakes sparkle like diamonds bright,
Caught in the glimmer of fragile light.
The stillness speaks, a sacred hush,
In the glare, all things seem to blush.

Bare trees shiver in the cool breeze,
Whispers of winter dancing through leaves.
And the sky wears a cloak of soft grey,
As the sun fights to keep the darkness at bay.

This quiet moment, both sweet and rare,
Holds the weight of the world in its care.
Each breath of air, a story to tell,
In the silence, we find where we dwell.

So behold the glare of the pale sun,
A fleeting reminder that life is spun.
With every dawn, the cycle renews,
In the light, we find solace and clues.

Seasonal Indifference

Trees stand barren, stripped of their pride,
In the face of change, they silently bide.
Their roots dig deep in the frozen ground,
While whispers of autumn linger around.

Snowflakes fall with a gentle grace,
Blanketing earth in a cold embrace.
Yet life beneath start to stir and sigh,
In the heart of winter, hopes don't die.

Days grow longer as the cycle turns,
In every heart, a quiet yearn.
The seasons shift without a care,
Indifference reigns in the crisp, cold air.

Yet beneath this calm, a warmth can be found,
In the promise of life, lurking underground.
Each creature waits for the thaw to sing,
In the silence, all await the spring.

So let the seasons come and go,
In their indifference, life still flows.
For in this dance of snow and sun,
Every cycle whispers we are one.

Glacial Dreams

In the quiet of the night,
Whispers of ice take flight.
Stars twinkle in the fray,
Casting dreams upon the bay.

Chill winds sweep the land,
Crystals gleam, soft and grand.
Paths shrouded in moonlight,
Glacial whispers take their flight.

Rivers frozen, deep and clear,
Nature's canvas, stark and dear.
Silent echoes, time stands still,
In this frozen world, we fulfill.

Frozen visions dance around,
Every heartache wrapped and bound.
Through the cold, our hopes ignite,
In glacial dreams, the soul takes flight.

So let's wander in this realm,
Where frost and dreams overwhelm.
In the silence, we find grace,
In glacial dreams, our sacred space.

Beneath the Haze of Frost

Beneath the haze where frost does creep,
A world lies still, in slumber deep.
Each breath a whisper, cold and bright,
Nature wrapped in silvery light.

Branches dressed in icy lace,
Glisten softly, wintry grace.
Hidden secrets lie in wait,
Under frost, the heart's true fate.

Footsteps muted on the ground,
In this quiet, magic found.
Beneath the haze, dreams intertwine,
Painting visions, soft as wine.

The sun's shy rays, like gentle streams,
Break the dusk with warming beams.
Yet the cold keeps shadows near,
Beneath the haze, whispers clear.

Hold this moment, treasure tight,
In the frosty glow of light.
Beneath the haze of frost we see,
Life's gentle dance, eternally free.

Frostflower Serenade

In the garden of ice and snow,
Frostflowers bloom, a gentle glow.
Petals shimmer under starlight,
Whispers soft in the frosty night.

Dancing shadows, shiver, sway,
In a serenade of frozen play.
Each bloom a story, tales unfold,
Of love and loss, of dreams retold.

Moonlight bathes the frosted ground,
Nature's whispers, a haunting sound.
In the silence, hearts align,
Frostflowers sway, a dance divine.

Beneath the sky of crystal dreams,
Where echoes linger, softly gleam.
A melody wrapped in frost's embrace,
Frostflower serenade, a sacred space.

So listen close to the night's refrain,
As frostflowers sing through joy and pain.
In their grace, we find our way,
In this serenade, forever stay.

When Shadows Freeze

When shadows freeze in twilight's breath,
Silent moments embrace the death.
Every heartbeat, a fragile thread,
In the realm where the cold is spread.

Ghostly figures dance in line,
Chilled laughter echoes, bittersweet wine.
Through the night, the frost will creep,
As dreams converge into the deep.

Stars above like diamonds twirl,
In the silence, visions swirl.
Time suspended, moments trapped,
In the dance of shadows wrapped.

Within the cold, our secrets lie,
Dreams igniting, reaching high.
When shadows freeze, we find our way,
In the stillness, night turns to day.

Hold this vision close and tight,
As shadows glide into the night.
When shadows freeze, our hearts unite,
In the story woven by moonlight.

Silent Snowfall

Gentle flakes descend so slow,
Wrapping earth in purest glow.
Whispers carried on the breeze,
Nature sighs with tranquil ease.

Each flake tells a silent tale,
In this hush where dreams unveil.
Footprints lost beneath the white,
Creating peace on winter's night.

Trees adorned in crystal lace,
In this stillness, find your place.
Stars peer through the cloudy veil,
As the world begins to pale.

Every flurry brings the hush,
In the night's enchanting rush.
Breathe the magic, feel the grace,
Snowflakes dance in soft embrace.

Permafrost Poetry

Beneath the ice, a secret lay,
Stories told of yesterday.
Frozen whispers, time stands still,
Nature's art, a silent thrill.

Cracks and crevices reveal,
Mysteries that time can heal.
Silent strength in every fold,
Permafrost, a tale of old.

Roots entwined in lasting sleep,
Hold the dreams that memories keep.
Life emerges, brave and bold,
In the tales that earth has told.

Each layer speaks of seasons past,
Tokens of the cold amassed.
In this realm, resilience grows,
Where the frozen river flows.

Winter's Lament

Bitter winds weave through the trees,
Singing songs of winter's freeze.
Empty branches reach up high,
Mourning under the gray sky.

Frosted breath upon the air,
Echoes of a world laid bare.
Moments lost in fleeting days,
Wrapped in white, a silent maze.

Shadows dance on fields of white,
Visions blurred, a soft twilight.
Memories of warmth long gone,
Frozen dreams of early dawn.

In the quiet, hearts entwine,
Waiting for the sun to shine.
Yet, within the chill's embrace,
Lies the beauty in its grace.

Echoes in the Frost

Silent echoes through the glade,
Frosty patterns softly laid.
Nature holds its breath in quiet,
Wrapped in winter's cool diet.

Footfalls crunch on snowy ground,
In this stillness, peace is found.
Whispers of the past unfold,
In the frost, a story told.

Icicles hang like chandeliers,
Glimmering through the passing years.
Every glint, a memory shines,
Carved in ice, as time aligns.

Above, the sky a slate-lid gray,
Softly hints at spring someday.
Yet for now, this chill remains,
In the echoes of winter's chains.

Frozen Whispers

In the stillness, secrets lie,
Snowflakes drift from a cloudy sky.
Silent breaths in the icy air,
Whispers soft, floating without care.

Trees stand tall in a cloak of white,
Guardians of stories, shunning light.
Branches creak like lullabies,
Nature's hush, as the cold wind sighs.

Footsteps crunch on a frosted path,
Echoing dreams, a quiet wrath.
In this world where time stands still,
Frozen moments, a gentle thrill.

Eyes closed tight, feeling the peace,
Fragments of warmth that never cease.
In each flake, a tale unfolds,
A dance of dreams in the winter's hold.

As shadows grow long and fade away,
Night embraces the dying day.
Stars awaken, a silver gleam,
Frozen whispers, a timeless dream.

Shards of Time

Fractured moments, lost and found,
Echoes trapped in the past's sound.
Glimmers of what once was clear,
Shattered glass, yet so near.

Time slips through our grasping hands,
Drifting like fine golden sands.
Memories linger, sweet and rife,
In the shadows of our life.

Fleeting glances, a stolen smile,
Remnants held for just a while.
Fragments dance in the twilight glow,
Reality bends, where dreams grow.

The clock ticks on, relentless plight,
Chasing moments into the night.
Yet in each shard, a story tells,
Of love and loss, where longing dwells.

As time will weave its silent rhyme,
We gather pieces, toe the line.
In every shard, a heartbeats' trace,
A mosaic of life, a sacred space.

Crystal Reflections

In the stillness, mirrors gleam,
Capturing light in a distant dream.
Fractals dance in brilliant hue,
A kaleidoscope of the old and new.

Each crystal holds a secret deep,
A promise of whispers, a bond to keep.
In every facet, stories blend,
Reflections of time that never end.

Shards of feeling twinkling bright,
Guiding lost souls through the night.
They shimmer gently, a soft glow,
Revealing paths we long to know.

Flickers of joy, of heartache past,
In the crystal's grasp, shadows cast.
Each gleam a memory, vivid and bold,
A timeless journey waiting to unfold.

As the dawn breaks on this jeweled shore,
Reflections call us to seek once more.
In the light of day, we'll find our way,
Through crystal visions that forever stay.

Frigid Echoes

In the silence, whispers play,
Frigid echoes of yesterday.
Frozen thoughts in the winter's breath,
Carried softly, a song of death.

Through bare branches, shadows creep,
Secrets buried, dreams to keep.
In the depths of frostbound ground,
Life's soft murmurs still resound.

With every gust, a tale unfolds,
Of forgotten times and brave hearts bold.
Echoes linger in the pale twilight,
Haunting the edges of the night.

A single tear on a snow-white ground,
An echo of laughter, lost but found.
Cold and stark, yet deeply felt,
In frigid whispers, the heart can melt.

As stars above in silence gleam,
They listen closely to every dream.
In the chill of night, life still glows,
Frigid echoes, where love still flows.

Shadows in Crystal

In the hall of whispered light,
Shadows dance with unseen grace,
Crystal shards in starry night,
Echoes of a fleeting trace.

Glimmers fade in twilight's breath,
Silent stories intertwine,
Each a fragment, life and death,
Captured in the glassy line.

Veils of mist shroud every glance,
Fleeting moments, soft and slow,
In their silence, shadows prance,
Where the crystal tides will flow.

With each turn, a secret told,
Reflections of forgotten dreams,
Carved in ice, both young and old,
Time unfurls its quiet schemes.

As the night begins to wane,
Shadows linger, bold yet shy,
In their dance, we find the pain,
Underneath the vast, cold sky.

A Time for Gleaming Stillness

In the hush of morning light,
Stillness breathes a quiet song,
Gleaming moments, pure and bright,
Where the heart feels it belongs.

Waves of calm caress the day,
Time slows down to gently breathe,
In this space, the mind will play,
Moments cherished, never sheathed.

Each reflection finds its peace,
Floating softly on the air,
In stillness, worries cease,
Captured in a moment's care.

Nature whispers secrets true,
In the glow of sunlit beams,
Every leaf a tale anew,
Laced with tender, fragile dreams.

As shadows stretch, the day will fade,
Stillness lingers on the breeze,
In this pause, our fears are laid,
Embraced by tranquil, whispered ease.

Winter's Lament

Frosted breath upon the air,
Winter weeps in silent night,
Every branch a somber care,
Shimmering in pale moonlight.

Blankets white on weary ground,
Crisp and cold, the world stands still,
Nature's voice, a muted sound,
Echoes of its frozen will.

In the chill, the heart feels tight,
Memories of warmth and gold,
Longing for that gentle light,
Wrapped in stories left untold.

Yet in darkness, beauty lies,
Every flake a tiny dream,
Sparkling under starlit skies,
Winter's sorrow, soft, it seems.

With each breath of whistling breeze,
Hope arises, blooms anew,
For in stillness, hearts find ease,
Winter's lament, ever true.

Fractured Reflections

In the mirror's shattered glass,
Fleeting images collide,
Lost in dreams that cannot pass,
Where the heart can't choose to hide.

Layers deep of fractured years,
Stories woven, torn apart,
Through the pain, we cast our fears,
Echoes of a restless heart.

Fragments catch the light of day,
Glancing truths, a hidden line,
In the chaos, we find play,
Fate and fortune intertwine.

Every shard a tale to tell,
Beneath the surface, shadows creep,
In the silence, secrets dwell,
Promises we struggle to keep.

Yet in pieces, beauty glows,
Each reflection tells its tale,
Through the cracks, our spirit flows,
Finding strength where we might pale.

Glacial Dreams

In the stillness, whispers freeze,
Where shadows dance among the trees.
Soft crystals glint in twilight's glow,
As time moves slow, like falling snow.

Hushed glades hold secrets untold,
Wrapped in blankets of silver and gold.
The moonlight weaves a tapestry bright,
Painting visions of endless night.

Winds carry tales of long ago,
Of frozen rivers and stars aglow.
Each breath a mist, a fleeting sigh,
Evoking dreams that linger nigh.

In frosty air, hopes take flight,
Chasing the echoes of pure delight.
With every star that breaks the dark,
A promise made, a tender spark.

Yet dawn will come, the thaw will break,
Melting dreams and hearts awake.
But in the cold depths, we shall find,
The lasting chill of a frozen mind.

Chilled Moments

Frost blankets fields in quiet grace,
Each flake a kiss on nature's face.
The world transforms in winter's glow,
Moments suspended, time moves slow.

Bare branches reach for the pale sky,
As icy winds begin to sigh.
Footprints crunch on the pristine white,
Marking paths in the soft twilight.

A fire crackles, warmth contained,
While outside, the frosty veil remained.
Gathered close, our thoughts alive,
In these chilled moments, we revive.

Cup of cocoa, steam in the air,
Soft laughter shared, free from despair.
Within the hush, deep bonds we weave,
In winter's grip, we choose to believe.

Each fleeting glance, a memory made,
In chilly breaths, our fears evade.
As snowflakes fall, we'll always find,
In every chill, love intertwined.

A Dance of Frost

Underneath the moon's soft gaze,
The world adorned in frosty haze.
A dance unfolds, silent and light,
Nature twirls in the shimmering night.

Each crystal flake tells a story clear,
Of whispered dreams that draw us near.
Branches sway in the gentle breeze,
As cold melodies drift through the trees.

With every step, the earth holds its breath,
In this ballet, we find no death.
Instead a birth of moments rare,
Where every flake floats down with care.

Shadows pirouette and glide,
In this wintry ballroom, we abide.
The chill invites us to partake,
In the sacred rhythms that we make.

So let us join this waltz of grace,
Embrace the cold, our fears erase.
For in this dance, we are alive,
In frost's embrace, our spirits thrive.

Winter's Embrace

Wrapped in layers, warm and snug,
Seeking solace, a gentle hug.
The world outside, a canvas bright,
Painted in whites, a pure delight.

Snowflakes swirl like dreams of old,
Silent stories waiting to unfold.
Footsteps echo on frosty ground,
In winter's grasp, magic is found.

With every chill, a comfort grows,
In hearthside whispers, love overflows.
As night descends, the stars ignite,
Guiding hearts through the serene night.

Hot drinks steaming, laughter shared,
In the cold, our souls are bared.
The warmth within is fiercely bright,
Against the winter's cool twilight.

So here we stand, hand in hand,
In winter's embrace, forever we stand.
With every season, more we crave,
The grace of cold, a heart so brave.

Secrets Beneath the Ice

Whispers swirl beneath the frost,
Silent tales of all that's lost.
Shadows dance on frozen streams,
Carrying the weight of dreams.

Crystals gleam in moonlit night,
Secrets hide from morning light.
Nature guards what lies beneath,
A world of calm, a frozen wreath.

Echoes linger, soft and pale,
Tracing stories in the veil.
Time stands still where cold winds blow,
Chilling thoughts that dwell below.

Footsteps crunch on snowy ground,
In the silence, truths are found.
Beneath the ice, life waits and hides,
In the depths, where mystery resides.

Seasons turn, but still it stays,
Holding fast to ancient ways.
With every thaw, old tales arise,
Yet some remain 'neath frozen skies.

Twilight in the Frost

As daylight fades, the chill sets in,
Twilight whispers where dreams begin.
A canvas painted in shades of gray,
Night's embrace keeps the cold at bay.

Trees stand tall with icy crowns,
Nature sleeps while the world drowns.
Stars begin to twinkle bright,
Heralding the silent night.

Frosty breath upon the air,
Shimmers softly, pure and rare.
In the stillness, hearts align,
Underneath the faded pine.

Shadows stretch, the moon does rise,
Bathing all in silver guise.
Whispers roam through this hushed space,
Finding warmth in winter's grace.

In the twilight, time stands still,
Moments linger, yet we feel.
Frosted dreams in gentle light,
Wrapping secrets through the night.

Haunting Winter Solstice

On the solstice night so black,
Shadows dance, no light to track.
The longest hours stretch their hands,
Embracing dark in silent lands.

Whispers echo through the trees,
Olden tales carried by the breeze.
Fires burn low, but spirits rise,
In the warmth, the ancient cries.

Veils of frost upon the ground,
Nature's breath, a haunting sound.
Underneath the starry veil,
Where the echoes tell the tales.

In this night of darkest dreams,
Hope will flicker, dimmer gleams.
Through the long and bitter cold,
We seek truth in stories told.

Yet dawn will break, as shadows fade,
Promises linger, never strayed.
On the solstice, hearts awaken,
Life returns, and fears are shaken.

Shattered Reflections

In the glassy lake, I see my face,
Flickers caught in a quiet space.
Ripples dance with every breath,
Silent whispers of life and death.

Fragments scatter with the breeze,
Echoes linger, lost with ease.
Each reflection a haunting truth,
Carving lines of forgotten youth.

Shadows fade, the night descends,
In the dark, the silence bends.
Memories ripple like the tide,
Carrying secrets we cannot hide.

Through the shards of broken light,
Stories shimmer in the night.
Every view, a piece of soul,
Searching for what makes us whole.

Yet beneath the fractured glass,
Lies a beauty none can pass.
In the depths, our spirits rise,
Revealing strength in quiet sighs.

Shimmering Veil

A whisper flows through twilight's glow,
Beneath the stars, a dance we know.
Veils of light in soft embrace,
Tracing dreams in cosmic space.

Glimmers fade in dawn's warm rise,
Colors shift beneath the skies.
In fleeting moments, magic sways,
Life's soft secrets weave their ways.

With every breath, the night unfolds,
Stories sung that time beholds.
A tapestry of shadows bright,
Kisses wrapped in silken light.

Beneath the shimmering veil we stand,
Boundless wonder, life unplanned.
In every shimmer, hope prevails,
Our hearts ignited, love unveils.

Icy Veins

Chill of winter lingers deep,
In silent nights, the secrets keep.
Frosted whispers touch the skin,
Shivering tales of where we've been.

Through haunted woods where shadows play,
Echoes freeze, and dreams betray.
In the heart, a cold refrain,
Hopes like crystals, sharp and plain.

Yet in the dark, a fire glows,
A warmth that only the brave knows.
Through icy veins, resilience flows,
A truth that only winter shows.

Each breath a frost, yet still we chase,
The fleeting warmth of love's embrace.
Through icy paths, we find our way,
Together, come what may.

The Stillness Between Heartbeats

In moments where the silence breathes,
Life's pulse rests beneath the leaves.
Between the beats, a world alive,
In quiet dance, our spirits thrive.

A pause that lingers, soft and deep,
Carved in echoes, secrets keep.
Within the hush, the soul takes flight,
Time suspends, a gentle light.

Every heartbeat, a whispered vow,
In stillness, we discover how.
Between each thrum, a chance to dream,
Life's essence flows, a silver stream.

Embracing voids where stillness swells,
Stories borne in silent bells.
In the stillness, we clearly see,
The magic lives within the free.

Frigid Reflections

Beneath the ice, the world is still,
Frozen dreams that time can't kill.
Mirrors of the past unwind,
In frigid depths, our dreams confined.

Sparks of life in crystal bounds,
Whispers echo, haunting sounds.
Reflections dance with frost and light,
In the shiver, we find our fight.

Each icy shard, a memory clear,
Breath of winter, calm yet near.
In solitude, our thoughts collide,
Truth emerges, heart opened wide.

Through frigid waters, courage flows,
In twilight's grasp, the spirit grows.
Amidst the chill, we find our way,
Frigid reflections hold the sway.

Hushed Crystals

In the stillness of the night,
Crystals glimmer under moonlight.
Whispers dance on icy air,
Silent secrets everywhere.

Snowflakes fall with gentle grace,
Covering the world's embrace.
Each a story, soft and bright,
Wrapped in winter's pure delight.

Trees stand tall with frosted crowns,
Casting shadows on the grounds.
In this wonderland of white,
Nature holds its breath so tight.

Breezes hum a soft refrain,
Chilly kisses, sweet as rain.
Hushed, the world begins to dream,
Underneath the silver beam.

Time stands still in diamond light,
Every moment feels so right.
In this realm of frozen sighs,
Beauty dwells beneath the skies.

Glacial Moments

Moments carved in ice and snow,
Whispers of the winds that blow.
Frozen dreams, a breath away,
In the dawn of winter's day.

Mountains wear their blankets white,
Veils of frost in morning light.
Every creak and crack denotes,
Secrets that the silence coats.

Rivers slow to quiet streams,
Hushed by winter's muted dreams.
Time is caught in frozen flow,
As the stillness starts to glow.

Flakes of wonder, pure and bright,
Caught in a soft, sparkling flight.
Nature's magic, crisp and clear,
Glacial moments, held so dear.

In each breath, a story lies,
Frosted scenes beneath the skies.
Life stands still, yet feels alive,
In this world, our hearts revive.

Windows of Winter

Through the panes, a world is set,
Windows framed in icy fret.
Each a glimpse of silent grace,
Winter's touch on every face.

Frosted patterns, lace so fine,
Nature's art, a pure design.
Breathless nights, the stars ignite,
In the chill, there glows a light.

Birds at rest, their songs concealed,
In this quiet, joys revealed.
Soft the glow of fireside dreams,
Warmth that flows in cozy streams.

Outside, the world in gentle sleep,
Inside, memories we keep.
Every window tells a tale,
Of winter's love that will not fail.

Time glides through the frosted gaze,
Moments wrapped in snowy haze.
Through these frames, we see the truth,
In winter's heart, there dwells our youth.

Frosted Whispers

Whispers flutter through the trees,
Carried softly by the breeze.
Frosted leaves like voices sigh,
Echoes of the winter sky.

Every flake a gentle note,
On the air, they drift and float.
Nature's melody unfolds,
In the whispers, tales are told.

Moonlit nights with silver sheen,
Glisten on the tranquil scene.
Stars are scattered, dreams take flight,
In the depth of frosty night.

In the hush, we find our peace,
Winter's calm brings sweet release.
Frosted whispers, soft and clear,
Holding all that we hold dear.

Through each breath, the cold air sings,
Winter's heart, a gift it brings.
In the still, where magic lies,
Frosted whispers touch the skies.

Snow Cloaked Secrets

Whispers in the silent night,
Snowflakes dance in soft moonlight.
Every hush a secret kept,
In the dark where shadows leapt.

Trees don cloaks of purest white,
While the stars twinkle so bright.
Footprints trace a fleeting path,
Nature's soft, enchanting wrath.

Beneath the snow, the world sleeps,
In dreams where the silence keeps.
Time stands still in calm embrace,
Hidden wonders find their place.

A veil of frost on branches bare,
Cloaked in beauty, unaware.
Winter's breath in every flake,
Tales of wonder it will make.

In this realm of chilly dreams,
Life is woven through the seams.
Snow cloaked secrets, pure and deep,
In the night, the world will weep.

Breath of Winter

Crisp and clear, the air is still,
Winter's breath on every hill.
Softly whispers through the trees,
Carrying a gentle freeze.

Pine trees wear their frosty crowns,
Laying low their heavy frowns.
Nature holds its breath in awe,
Life stands still, a silent draw.

Frozen lakes reflect the sky,
Clouds drift slowly, floating by.
Every shimmer tells a tale,
Of winter's magic in the pale.

In the night, the stars align,
As the world, it starts to shine.
Underneath the silver glow,
Heartfelt warmth begins to flow.

Embrace the stillness all around,
In this peace, our hearts are found.
Breath of winter, crisp and clear,
A season's hymn we hold so dear.

Ephemeral Chill

A fleeting touch of winter's kiss,
Moments caught in quiet bliss.
Breath of cold against the skin,
Whispers of where dreams begin.

Snowflakes fall like gentle sighs,
Painting earth beneath the skies.
Every flake, a story spun,
Ephemeral, yet all as one.

Frigid winds might bid us stay,
In the dusk, where shadows play.
Frosted breath in the twilight air,
Nature speaks, the world laid bare.

Time stands still in winter's grasp,
Holding tight in its tender clasp.
Golden warmth may fade away,
Yet in chill, we find our way.

Ephemeral chill, soft and light,
Guides us through the deep of night.
In the silence, hearts collide,
With the beauty found inside.

Frosted Horizons

Beyond the hills, where silence reigns,
Frosted horizons hold their chains.
Misty mornings, crisp and bright,
Dawn's embrace, a pure delight.

Glistening snow on every peak,
Nature hides the words we seek.
In the stillness, magic brews,
Every moment painted new.

Icicles hang like frozen tears,
Holding tales from distant years.
Each reflection whispers low,
Tales of winter's ancient glow.

As the sun begins to rise,
Colors dance beneath the skies.
Frosted air, a gentle thrill,
In the quiet, hearts can fill.

Frosted horizons, wide and grand,
Life unfolds at winter's hand.
Embrace the chill, feel the grace,
In this realm, we find our place.

Lament of the Frozen Heart

In shadows deep where silence weeps,
The frozen heart in solitude sleeps.
Amidst the ice, the echoes cry,
A love once warm, now lost but nigh.

With every breath, the chill draws near,
Lost whispers fade, they disappear.
The winter's hold, a bitter pain,
Reminds the heart of love's disdain.

Through icy winds, a mournful song,
Of memories where I belong.
Once vibrant flames now flicker dim,
A love that danced on winter's whim.

Yet in the night, a spark appears,
Amidst the frost, it stirs my fears.
Can warmth return to thaw this chill?
Or shall the heart succumb to still?

In frozen dreams, I search for light,
To melt away this endless night.
For in the heart, a glimmer stays,
Of love that fought through winter's maze.

Frosted Moonlit Dreams

Under moonlight, pale and bright,
Frosted dreams take wing in flight.
Whispers dance on winter's breath,
A gentle touch, a sweet caress.

Stars align in velvet skies,
As snowflakes fall like whispered sighs.
In quietude, the world sleeps sound,
In frosted glades where peace is found.

Through the night, the shadows play,
As dreams unfold in soft ballet.
Each sparkling flake, a wish untold,
In moonlit warmth, our hearts grow bold.

With every heartbeat, stars ignite,
Guiding souls through winter's night.
In twilight's glow, our spirits soar,
Frosted dreams forevermore.

In this realm, where magic weaves,
The tapestry of winter leaves.
Love blooms under celestial schemes,
In the embrace of frosted dreams.

Echoes of Snow-laden Stillness

In quiet woods where silence reigns,
Snow-laden branches hold the pains.
Whispers float on frosty air,
Echoes linger, unaware.

Footsteps soft on carpets white,
Nature's stillness, pure delight.
Echoing sounds of peace abound,
A frozen symphony resounds.

Each flake a memory from the past,
In winter's hold, I find contrast.
The world transformed, a crystal glaze,
In this stillness, I find my gaze.

Beneath the stars, a hush prevails,
As winter tells its ancient tales.
In snow-clad realms, my heart finds peace,
In echoes soft, my worries cease.

As morning breaks, the sun will gleam,
Awakening the frozen dream.
Yet in my heart, the echoes stay,
Of snow-laden stillness, come what may.

Delicate Dance of Winter's Grasp

In twilight's glow, the world transforms,
A delicate dance, the spirit warms.
With every flake that gently falls,
Winter's grasp, a silent call.

Frosty breath upon my skin,
The dance begins, a waltz within.
Each movement soft, a tender trace,
In winter's arms, a soft embrace.

The nights unfold like silken thread,
Where dreams are spun and gently spread.
In this ballet of crisp delight,
We twirl beneath the starlit night.

As shadows blend with silvery light,
The world is veiled in purest white.
In this moment, joy aligns,
In winter's dance, our hearts entwined.

So let us move with gentle grace,
As winter's whisper finds its place.
In every step, the music calls,
A delicate dance that never falls.

Crystalized Days

In morning light, the frost appears,
A world awake, as nature cheers.
Each crystal formed, a fleeting dream,
Time captured in a silver beam.

Through the trees, the whispers glide,
Past moments held, we cannot hide.
With each breath, we find a way,
To cherish all our crystalized days.

The sun will rise, the shadows fall,
In every joy, in every call.
Life's fragile treasures shine so bright,
Illuminated by soft light.

Yet seasons turn, and so must we,
Embrace the change, and let it be.
For in the glass, our stories lay,
Forever etched in crystalized day.

So hold it close, this fleeting bliss,
In tender moments, do not miss.
Life's beauty captured, come what may,
In the heart of each crystalized day.

Flickering Glimmers

In the dark, a light appears,
Flickering soft, it calms our fears.
Whispers of hope, like stars align,
Guiding us through the night divine.

Each glimmer sparkles, pure and bright,
In shadows cast, it brings us light.
With every flicker, dreams arise,
Painting the world in soft disguise.

Through aching hearts and silent tears,
We find the strength that perseveres.
Little by little, step by step,
In fleeting moments, promises kept.

So let us dance in the glow,
With flickering glimmers, let love flow.
For in the dark, we find our way,
Guided by hope, come what may.

Together we'll stand, hand in hand,
In the flickers, we make our stand.
Embrace the magic, the dawn's embrace,
Flickering glimmers, our sacred space.

Shattering Stillness

In the silence, echoes break,
Shattering stillness, dreams awake.
A distant sound, a whispered call,
As shadows dance upon the wall.

Still waters hide a stormy heart,
Ripples forming, tearing apart.
With every breath, we feel the strain,
A pause before the gentle rain.

Yet beauty lies beneath the noise,
In fragile bonds, in simple joys.
We gather strength through trials faced,
In shattered stillness, love is traced.

Through cracks of light, our spirits soar,
Embracing life, forevermore.
In chaos found, we find our place,
Shattering stillness, a warm embrace.

So let the echoes freely flow,
In the quiet, together we'll grow.
For in the stillness, we shall find,
A love that breaks through, intertwined.

Shimmering Hourglass

The sands of time begin to fall,
In shimmering hues, we heed the call.
Moments slipping, hard to grasp,
In the hourglass, we tightly clasp.

Every grain tells a story told,
Of laughter bright and love so bold.
With each tick, our lives unfold,
In shimmering light, our dreams are sold.

Yet as we watch the time move on,
We find our strength, though days seem long.
In twilight's glow, we pause to see,
The beauty in life's tapestry.

So let us cherish every part,
Embrace the moments, hold each heart.
Time may shimmer, quickly pass,
But love remains, the greatest mass.

In the hourglass, we dance and play,
Through fleeting hours, we find our way.
So let it shine, this golden hour,
As dreams dissolve, yet love is power.

Quietude in the Chill

In the hush of winter's breath,
Softly falling, the world beneath,
A tranquil scene, serene and bright,
Embracing peace in the pale night.

Branches crowned with frosted lace,
Whispers echo, a gentle grace,
Stars above in their frozen dance,
Invite the heart to take a chance.

The moon casts shadows long and lean,
On fields of white, a silent sheen,
With every step, a crunch that's sweet,
Winter's calm beneath our feet.

The air, so crisp, will clear the mind,
In quietude, we seek and find,
A moment's pause, a breath, a sigh,
In the chill, our thoughts may fly.

So linger here, let time stand still,
Embrace the night with heart and will,
In the stillness, let worries cease,
For in this chill, we find our peace.

Dance of the Icy Veil

Beneath the trees, a frosty show,
The snowflakes twirl, a waltzing flow,
Nature spins in a silver light,
A dance of calm in the still night.

Each flake descends, a unique grace,
Covering earth in a soft embrace,
A symphony of whispers and sighs,
As winter dons her soft disguise.

The wind joins in with a gentle tune,
Swaying branches 'neath the moon,
In the chill, we're beckoned near,
To join this dance, amide the cheer.

With every breath, the magic grows,
Embracing warmth in the icy prose,
Where laughter mingles with the cold,
In stories shared and warmth retold.

So lift your heart, let yourself glide,
In warmth and joy, let love preside,
For in this dance, we find our way,
Through the icy veil, come what may.

Breath of Winter's Night

When twilight falls and stars ignite,
Breath of winter whispers bright,
Chill settles in with a gentle sway,
Guiding dreams where shadows play.

The world adorned in crystal hues,
Offers magic in every view,
In silent nights, the wonders flow,
As icy winds begin to blow.

Crimson embers in the hearth,
Warm the soul, ignite the heart,
While outside, blankets thickly lay,
Guarding secrets of the day.

The moonlit path calls to explore,
Through frozen woods forevermore,
Beckoning hearts to venture forth,
Amidst the chill, we find our worth.

So breathe the night, feel the embrace,
Of winter's breath, a soft caress,
In its coolness, life anew,
Awakens magic, tried and true.

Threads of Cold Interwoven

In tapestry of white and grey,
Threads of cold gently sway,
Woven stories in the frost,
Of warmth and wonder, never lost.

Each glistening strand holds a tale,
Of journeys taken, paths that hail,
In winter's loom, we find our place,
Interwoven hearts in a soft embrace.

The world transformed in icy grace,
Hopes and dreams in this sacred space,
As every breath forms a cloud,
In the chill, we sing out loud.

The beauty found in the fleeting cold,
In every moment, life unfolds,
With every flake that twirls and spins,
New adventures of warmth begins.

So gather close, let stories flow,
In winter's grace, let your heart glow,
For in these threads, both frail and bold,
We find connections, treasures untold.

Ghosts of Winter

Whispers dance on icy breath,
Shadows cloaked in frosty death.
Silent trees, their branches bare,
Winter's grip hangs in the air.

Nights so long, the stars take flight,
Fires cast a warm, soft light.
Echoes of the past still roam,
In the cold, they find their home.

Footprints lost in fallen snow,
Where the frozen rivers flow.
Time stands still beneath the moon,
Ghosts of winter hum their tune.

Memories wrapped in flannel nights,
Hearts ignited by the sights.
Stories whisper like the winds,
In the chill, a warmth begins.

Yet the dawn will break the chill,
Seasons change and hearts will fill.
But the ghosts will linger near,
Haunting winter, crystal clear.

Transient Frost

Morning glimmers, soft and light,
Transient frost, a fleeting sight.
Nature's art on blades of grass,
Delicate as moments pass.

Sunrise paints the world anew,
Golden rays, a warm debut.
Frost will fade, like dreams at dawn,
In this glow, life carries on.

Each crystal holds a secret kept,
In the chill, the earth has slept.
Melting whispers through the air,
Transience, a truth so rare.

Wind will weave through tree and thorn,
Carrying signs of early morn.
With each breath, we learn to trust,
Beauty lies in fleeting gusts.

As the day gives way to night,
Stars will twinkle, oh so bright.
Frost may vanish, yet we find,
Memories linger in the mind.

Shattered Seasons

Leaves fall like whispers to the ground,
Colors clash, their beauty drowned.
Winter's chill encircles tight,
Shattered seasons lose their light.

Once it danced in vibrant hues,
Now it fades in quiet blues.
Yearning for the sun's warm glow,
Hope still flickers, soft and slow.

Fragments of a dream once bright,
Shimmer in the fading light.
Nature grieves in muted tones,
A symphony of heartstone moans.

Moments lost in time's cruel spin,
Each breath whispers where we've been.
Yet beneath the frozen layer,
Life awaits, a brave prayer.

So we gather shards of grace,
Holding on in this wild space.
From shattered seasons, blooms arise,
Emerging beneath silent skies.

Breath of the North

Breezes whisper through the pines,
Nature hums in sacred lines.
The breath of North, both wild and free,
Calls to all, including me.

Mountains stand like ancient guards,
Claiming secrets, leaving shards.
Rivers sing with silver waves,
In their depths, the freedom braves.

Snowflakes twirl in crisp, cold air,
Dancing gently, without care.
Each breath taken, a promise made,
In the north, our fears may fade.

Stars emerge in velvet skies,
Winking down, ancient ties.
Beneath their gaze, our spirits soar,
In the stillness, we implore.

So let us wander, hearts held high,
In the shadows, where dreams lie.
Breath of the North, strong and pure,
Calls us home, forever sure.

Memories Encased in Frost

Whispers dance on winter's breath,
Frozen tales of love and death.
Each flake tells a story, bright,
In the stillness of the night.

Echoes wrapped in icy lace,
Moments trapped in time and space.
Silent screams and laughter lost,
All entwined in winter's frost.

Frosted windows, shadows cast,
Chasing memories from the past.
Footsteps lost beneath the chill,
Time stands still, yet hearts can thrill.

In the glint of morning light,
Frozen dreams take for their flight.
Gentle sighs of snowflakes fall,
In the silence, hear their call.

Memories in crystalline gleam,
Reflecting every distant dream.
In the frost, our hearts remain,
Kept alive amidst the pain.

White Silence

The world wrapped in quiet grace,
A blanket soft, a calming space.
Snowflakes flutter, whispers small,
In this moment, we hear their call.

Pine trees wear their coats of white,
Fields of diamonds, pure and bright.
Footsteps muffled, all is still,
Nature's breath, a gentle thrill.

Clouds hang low in misty veils,
Carrying tales on winter trails.
Silence reigns, a cherished gift,
As time drifts slowly in its lift.

The air is crisp, a sweet caress,
In this peace, we find our rest.
Moments linger, soft and grand,
In white silence, hand in hand.

Each heartbeat echoes like a song,
In this kingdom where we belong.
Dreams are woven into night,
Embraced in soft, serene white.

A Glimpse of the Glacial Realm

Crystal mountains, sharp and bright,
Glisten softly in the light.
Rivers flow, their icy dance,
Each ripple holds a fleeting chance.

Frozen echoes fill the air,
In a realm that's bold and rare.
Nature's canvas, vast and wide,
In glacial shadows, secrets hide.

The sun dips low, the sky ablaze,
Colors melt in fleeting haze.
A silence wraps the vast expanse,
In awe, we lose ourselves in chance.

Tales of ages carved in stone,
Whisper softly, not alone.
Glimmers shine in twilight's gleam,
A glacial realm where dream meets dream.

Footprints mark the snowy ground,
In solitude, we're glory-bound.
A glimpse of beauty, fierce and grand,
In nature's heart, we understand.

Quiet Shadows on Ice

Beneath the stars, shadows creep,
Silent whispers, secrets keep.
Ice reflects the midnight glow,
Where the frozen rivers flow.

Footsteps echo on the lake,
In the stillness, silence breaks.
Nature's breath, a soft embrace,
In the shadows, find our place.

Moonlit paths, a shining dance,
In this stillness, hearts advance.
Stars descend with gentle grace,
Painting dreams on winter's face.

Each breath rises in the cold,
Stories whispered, yet untold.
Quiet moments, treasures found,
In this space, we're glory-bound.

The world fades to shades of night,
In the dark, we find our light.
With quiet shadows, dreams align,
In ice-bound stillness, hearts entwine.

A Winter's Cradle

In a blanket of white,
The world rests so still,
Soft whispers of night,
As dreams start to fill.

Branches draped with lace,
Stars twinkle above,
Each flake falls with grace,
A sign of pure love.

The moon's gentle glow,
Guides the quiet earth,
In silence we know,
Of hope and rebirth.

Footprints trace a path,
In the cold, crisp air,
Hearts warm from the math,
Of moments we share.

Let us hold this peace,
In our hearts so tight,
Winter's sweet release,
A cradle of light.

Luminescent Frost

Frost kisses the morn,
A glimmering sight,
A new day is born,
In soft shades of white.

Trees wear their jewels,
As sunlight breaks through,
Nature's own tools,
To paint a view.

The air crisp and clear,
With whispers so light,
Each breath brings us near,
To magic in flight.

Footsteps crunch the ground,
In rhythm we dance,
A world wrapped around,
In winter's romance.

As day fades to night,
The stars start to gleam,
With frosty delight,
We dream and we dream.

Feathers of Snow

Feathers drift and glide,
From skies high above,
In silence they bide,
A message of love.

Softly they descend,
Like whispers in air,
Nature's own blend,
Of beauty so rare.

Each flake tells a tale,
Of weathered old skies,
With stories to hail,
That dance as they rise.

Children laugh with glee,
As snowballs take flight,
In this tranquil sea,
Of winter's delight.

Under the pale moon,
Night's blanket unfolds,
In winter's sweet tune,
Feathers grace our souls.

Clarity Beneath the Chill

The world breathes in cold,
With crystals that sing,
Of secrets retold,
As winter takes wing.

Branches stretch and sway,
With weight they now bear,
The sun's fading ray,
Leaves shadows laid bare.

Moments freeze in time,
In a world wrapped so tight,
Each heartbeat, a rhyme,
Against the soft night.

Trust the calm inside,
As chill wraps the ground,
In quiet, abide,
Where peace can be found.

When spring starts to rise,
It whispers, "Be still,"
For clarity flies,
Beneath every chill.

Ethereal Chill

In twilight's grip, the shadows play,
A silver mist where night holds sway.
The stars awake with gentle light,
In whispers soft, they greet the night.

A frozen breath upon the air,
Each crystal flake beyond compare.
The world transformed, a dreamlike trance,
With every glance, we take a chance.

In quiet groves, where silence dwells,
The echoes weave their fleeting spells.
A tranquil hush, the heart unfolds,
In afterglow, a tale retold.

As moonlight dances on the ground,
In nature's grasp, we feel unbound.
The night enfolds, a warm embrace,
In ethereal stillness, we find grace.

Amidst the chill, our spirits soar,
Awakening dreams we can't ignore.
With every breath, the night ignites,
An ethereal chill, a world of lights.

Frost-kissed Memories

Nostalgia breathes in frosty air,
Where time stands still, beyond compare.
The laughter echoes, soft and sweet,
In every corner, memories meet.

A blanket white on fields of gold,
The stories shared, the tales retold.
Each moment held in icy grasp,
Forever cherished, never past.

The frosted glass, a window frame,
Each crystal shard, a whispered name.
In shimmering lights, the past returns,
As winter's fire within us burns.

We wander pathways, quiet, slow,
Where frosty breath and memories flow.
In every step, a ghostly trace,
Of laughter lost in time and space.

Embracing all the joy and pain,
The frost-kissed echoes still remain.
In every heartbeat, every sigh,
Our memories dance beneath the sky.

Whispers on the Wind

The whispers ride on gentle breeze,
Soft secrets shared among the trees.
As twilight falls, they softly call,
In harmony, they weave through all.

The rustling leaves, a whispered song,
Invite us in where we belong.
With every breath, their voices climb,
We lose ourselves in fleeting time.

The nightingale's sweet serenade,
Among the stars, our fears allayed.
The moonlight dances, shadows sway,
As whispers guide our hearts today.

In every sigh, a tale unfolds,
Of love and dreams and fears untold.
The wind may carry all we'd share,
In whispers soft, beyond compare.

Through valleys deep and mountains high,
The breezes weave, they never die.
In every heart, a story penned,
With whispers on the wind, our friend.

Seasons of Silence

In quietude, the seasons tread,
Where time to pause and listen's led.
A gentle hush upon the land,
In silence, we begin to stand.

The autumn leaves, they softly fall,
Each color speaks, a final call.
Beneath the weight of snow and frost,
We find the peace in what was lost.

The winter's breath, a lullaby,
Where dreams take flight and spirits fly.
In frozen moments, hearts align,
In seasons of silence, we intertwine.

With spring, a whisper starts anew,
As blossoms bloom and skies turn blue.
The gentle stir of life's embrace,
In every step, we find our place.

Each fleeting season teaches slow,
The art of listening, letting go.
In every heartbeat, every sigh,
Seasons of silence teach us why.

Shimmering Silence

In the hush of night, stars gleam bright,
Whispers of dreams take their flight,
Moonbeams dance on quiet streams,
Wrapped in the warmth of silver beams.

Shadows drift and gently sway,
Embracing the magic of the gray,
Every breath a soft refrain,
In shimmering silence, peace we gain.

Petals fall, the world holds its breath,
Echoes linger in the depths,
Time pauses to catch its sigh,
In this stillness, we learn to fly.

With each heartbeat, a secret told,
Stories of hearts, both brave and bold,
In the night, where dreams reside,
Shimmering silence, our guide, our pride.

So let us wander through the dark,
Finding solace in this spark,
In the quiet, our souls entwine,
In shimmering silence, pure and divine.

Fractured Light

Through fractured glass, the sun breaks free,
Casting colors, wild and spree,
A prism of dreams, a spectrum of heart,
In every shard, a work of art.

Beneath the hues, the shadows play,
Whispers of night that stretch and sway,
A fleeting glimpse of what's concealed,
In fractured light, the truth revealed.

Echoes of laughter, a distant call,
Reflected joy in moments small,
Each flicker holds a tale untold,
In fractured light, we turn to gold.

Yet still, the world can seem so stark,
As darkness deepens, losing spark,
But through the cracks, we blend and fight,
Creating beauty in fractured light.

Let love illuminate the unknown,
Finding warmth in places grown,
A journey through chaos and plight,
In every crack, we find the light.

Time's Icy Grasp

Frozen moments, held so tight,
Glimmers of truth in the dead of night,
Time's icy fingers curl and bend,
Holding secrets that never end.

Each tick echoes in the chill,
Shadows dance with quiet thrill,
Seasons change with a hushed gasp,
Caught forever in time's icy grasp.

Memories like snowflakes fall,
Twisting, swirling, the past's soft call,
In frozen frames, we find our past,
Time's icy grasp, a spell that lasts.

Yet through the frost, a fire glows,
A warmth that in the heart still flows,
Breaking chains that time has cast,
In the struggle, a love vast.

So let us chase the fleeting year,
Embrace the warmth, overcome the fear,
For in this dance, we find our path,
Against time's icy grasp, we laugh.

Frostbitten Reverie

In the still of dawn, frost decorates,
Nature's canvas, beauty awaits,
Whispers of dreams float on the air,
In frostbitten reverie, we dare.

Every breath a fog, soft and light,
Moments captured, pure delight,
A chill that wraps round hearts so warm,
In fragile beauty, we find our charm.

Time seems to pause in this calm scene,
Echoing whispers of what might have been,
In every glimmer, memories we weave,
Frostbitten reverie, we believe.

So let us lose ourselves in the white,
Dancing shadows in morning light,
In this magic, our spirits soar,
Frostbitten reverie, forevermore.

With laughter ringing, we'll chase the day,
Embracing the frost in playful sway,
Each moment, a gift, pure and free,
In frostbitten reverie, you and me.

Frosty Memoirs

In the quiet hush of night,
Whispers dance on frozen air.
Memories wrapped in silver light,
Echoes linger everywhere.

Snowflakes fall like whispered dreams,
Each one tells a tale untold.
Glittering under moonlit beams,
A tapestry of winter's gold.

Footprints fade on paths of white,
Fleeting moments, soft and rare.
In the stillness, pure delight,
Frosty whispers softly share.

Beneath the stars, a tranquil glow,
Evening drapes in icy lace.
Time slows down, and all below,
Frosted memories find their place.

As dawn arrives with rosy hue,
Night retreats, yet leaves its mark.
In the heart, these moments brew,
Holding warmth within the dark.

Shivers of Twilight

As daylight dims, the chill descends,
Shadows stretch on glistening grass.
In twilight's glow, the cold transcends,
Nature whispers, seasons pass.

Crisp air tingles on the skin,
Colors fade to muted gray.
In this silence, we begin,
To ponder dusk's enchanted play.

Frosty breath and gentle sighs,
The world transforms in twilight's fold.
Underneath the painted skies,
Stories of the night unfold.

Stars awaken, bright and clear,
Each one like a wish set free.
The night wraps all in crystal sheer,
Embracing dreams and reverie.

In the still, a magic flows,
As darkness dances with the light.
In shivers, twilight's beauty grows,
A moment captured, pure delight.

Mists of Icy Reverie

In the morning light, a shroud,
Mists weave tales from dreams once made.
Icy fingers curl around,
Whispers of a night that stayed.

Frozen dew on blades of grass,
Nature's jewels, soft and rare.
Moments fleeting, yet they pass,
Carried gently in the air.

Echoes of a winter song,
In the stillness, secrets blend.
Mists arise where hearts belong,
Binding memories that won't end.

Each breath clouds in frosty air,
Painting visions, old and new.
Wrapped in reverie, we dare,
To wander where the mists ensue.

Through the haze, we find our path,
Guided by the softest light.
In this realm, we feel the wrath,
Of winter's breath, a sweet delight.

Frosted Paths Untraveled

Beneath a canopy of white,
We wander where few have stepped.
Frosted dreams in morning light,
Whispers of the roads we kept.

Each step crunches underfoot,
Leaving traces in the snow.
In this chill, our spirits hoot,
As the world around us glows.

Branches heavy, adorned with ice,
Nature's grace, a sparkling spree.
Hidden wonders, a true paradise,
Invite us forth, wild and free.

Paths untraveled call our name,
With every twist, a new delight.
In this realm, we play our game,
Chasing shadows, hearts take flight.

Through frosty woods, we roam and play,
The air thick with promise and cheer.
In every heartbeat, winter's sway,
Guides us onward with no fear.

Chill of Dusk

The sun dips low in the sky,
Casting shadows as it sighs.
Whispers of night begin to rise,
Cool winds tease, with gentle cries.

Stars emerge with a tender glow,
As the moon starts its quiet show.
Nature's hush begins to grow,
In the heart of dusk's soft flow.

A chill creeps on, a velvet thread,
Wraps the earth in quiet dread.
The vibrant hues of day widespread,
Fade to dreams as silence is bred.

Branches sway in the fading light,
As creatures hush, prepare for night.
Peaceful moments, a sweet invite,
In the arms of dusk, all feels right.

The world transforms in twilight's kiss,
A gentle murmur, a tranquil bliss.
In this stillness, time we won't miss,
Capturing magic, the hour's abyss.

Beneath Frosted Veils

Morning breaks, a soft embrace,
Each snowflake falls, time to trace.
Nature's quilt, a silvery lace,
Underneath, a hidden space.

Trees stand tall, in frosted thews,
Whispers of wind tell ancient truths.
Every branch wrapped tight in hues,
Of icy blue, an art that soothes.

A world so quiet, dreams ignite,
In the chill, a pure delight.
Footsteps crunch in soft twilight,
Wonders found in frost's invite.

Streams that freeze and then unbind,
Reflect the beauty, pure, unlined.
In this moment, peace you find,
Beneath the veils, the heart aligned.

The sun breaks through with golden rays,
Making diamonds in cold displays.
Nature's art, in glorious ways,
Frosted veils, the mind's sweet gaze.

A Symphony of Ice

Silent chords in the winter air,
Echo through the branches bare.
Notes of crispness, everywhere,
A symphony beyond compare.

Icicles hang, like crystal chimes,
Each droplet brings a flow of rhymes.
Nature's song in rhythm climbs,
In the cold, the joy primes.

Skates upon the frozen pond,
Draw lines of music, sweet and fond.
Every glide, a grace so blonde,
Melodies weave, as dreams respond.

Shadows dance like ghostly ties,
Underneath the moonlit skies.
Frozen landscapes, nature's sighs,
In the silence, beauty lies.

The world transforms, a sparkling face,
Every flake brings its own grace.
In icy halls, we find our place,
A symphony of time and space.

Hourglass of Frost

In the stillness, snowflakes fall,
An hourglass, enchanting call.
Time slows down, a gentle thrall,
Each moment held, a soft install.

Frozen streams and glistening trees,
Nature whispers on the breeze.
Counting moments with such ease,
In this calm, the spirit flees.

Wrapped in warmth, the hearth aglow,
Outside, the chill begins to grow.
Hours blend in a glittering show,
As frost collects with silent flow.

Count the beats of winter's song,
Through the quiet, we belong.
In the frost, we become strong,
Embracing time, where hearts prolong.

As night descends, we close our eyes,
Dreams take flight with starlit skies.
In the hourglass, fondness lies,
Frost reminds us, love never dies.

Murmurs of Crystal Clarity

In shadows soft, the whispers play,
A dance of light in the break of day.
Each crystal sound, a tale untold,
In silence deep, the heart feels bold.

Reflections gleam on waters wide,
Where truths emerge, and dreams abide.
A gentle touch upon the skin,
The world unfolds, it draws us in.

With every breath, the echoes rise,
A tapestry spun beneath the skies.
In every shimmer, a moment's grace,
The soul finds peace in this vast space.

Beneath the branches, secrets rest,
In nature's arms, we feel the best.
A symphony of soft delight,
Murmurs weaving through the night.

So let us wander, hand in hand,
Through realms of wonder, to understand.
With each soft murmur, hearts unite,
In crystal clarity, we take flight.

Solitude in Snow

In winter's embrace, the world is still,
A hush descends with a tranquil thrill.
White blankets cover the earth in peace,
As time stands still, and worries cease.

Footprints fade on the icy ground,
In solitude, a solace found.
The frosty air, a crisp delight,
Beneath the stars, the heart takes flight.

Each flake that falls, a whisper sweet,
Tells of dreams in the cold retreat.
A moment cherished, so pure, so bright,
In solitude, an inner light.

The trees stand tall, draped in white,
Guardians of this serene night.
While silence weaves its gentle shroud,
In solitude, I speak aloud.

So let the snowflakes dance and swirl,
In this stillness, I softly twirl.
With every breath, a new hope grows,
In solitude, my spirit glows.

Radiance of the Freeze

In frozen realms, brilliance gleams,
A landscape born of silver dreams.
Where frost adorns each branch and leaf,
The chill brings forth a quiet belief.

The world, a canvas of sparkling white,
Bathed in glow by the pale moonlight.
Each crystal formed in nature's mold,
A story whispered, a truth retold.

The icy breath of winter's grace,
Transforms the earth, a stunning face.
In every glitter, a promise lies,
A beauty caught beneath the skies.

As shadows lengthen, colors blend,
The sunset glows—a fiery end.
Yet in the freeze, there's warmth within,
For love and light help us begin.

So dance upon the frozen plain,
In radiance of the cold, we gain.
With hearts aglow, we face the freeze,
In winter's arms, our spirits ease.

The Shimmering Stillness

In the quiet realm where shadows rest,
A shimmering stillness, a moment blessed.
The gentle breeze, a comforting sigh,
As stars awaken in the midnight sky.

The world holds its breath, a tranquil pause,
In the midnight glow, we find our cause.
Each shimmering light, a guiding star,
Leading us close, no matter how far.

Beneath the moon, the whispers flow,
With every glance, the feelings grow.
In silence deep, our dreams take flight,
In shimmering stillness, all feels right.

The night's embrace, a soothing balm,
In the dimness, we feel the calm.
With every heartbeat, a timeless dance,
In stillness, we find our chance.

So let us linger, lost in the glow,
In shimmering stillness, our love will grow.
With hearts aligned in the quiet night,
Together we'll chase the morning light.

Time Crystalized

Moments captured in a glint,
A treasure lost in time's own print.
Silent echoes of the past,
Each memory, a shadow cast.

In the stillness, I behold,
Fragments of a tale retold.
Fleeting seconds, crystal clear,
Whispered wishes in the sphere.

Ticking clocks and spinning wheels,
The heart remembers how it feels.
Frozen nights and summer's dew,
Time's embrace, a soothing hue.

In the dance of shadows' play,
Moments weave in soft array.
Caught within this fleeting breath,
Life's tapestry, a quiet death.

Yet in each fragment, hope resides,
A glimmer where the spirit hides.
Time, elusive yet so close,
A crystal charm that we all chose.

Ethereal Frosted Light

Glistening under the moon's soft glow,
Frozen whispers through the trees do flow.
A delicate lace of frost adorned,
Nature's beauty, silently warmed.

Each flake a story from worlds afar,
Shimmering waves, a silver star.
Dancing sprites in the cold night's air,
Ethereal light, a dream to share.

Through gardens wrapped in winter's breath,
Life lies dormant, shrouded in death.
Yet underneath the icy sheet,
The pulse of life, a steady beat.

With every dawn, a new embrace,
Frosted forms start to interlace.
The sun ascends with brilliant might,
Awakening the frosted light.

In this moment, still and bright,
Magic breathes in pure delight.
Ethereal beauty, soft and kind,
A treasure in our hearts we find.

Celestial Whisper of Snow

Gentle flakes from heavens above,
A silent dance, a gift of love.
Whispers soft upon the ground,
In every flurry, peace is found.

Stars descend to kiss the earth,
In their touch, a tender mirth.
Cosmic secrets in the night,
Wrapped in snow, pure and white.

Each step muffled, time in pause,
Nature rests without a cause.
Calm and quiet reign supreme,
In this world, like a dream.

A tapestry of quiet grace,
Softly woven, a warm embrace.
Celestial echoes softly flow,
In the hush, the heart will grow.

Snowflakes linger, stories told,
In their beauty, we unfold.
Celestial worlds in twilight's glow,
A love that whispers with the snow.

Winter's Still Embrace

In winter's grasp, the world does sigh,
The trees stand tall, their branches nigh.
A quiet stretch of blankets white,
Night's cool kiss, a soft twilight.

Breath of frost adorns the air,
A stillness held in whispered prayer.
Each moment draped in silver light,
A canvas painted cold and bright.

Footfalls muffled, echoes flee,
In this hush, I find the key.
To moments lost and dreams regained,
In winter's hold, no heart is pained.

With every flake that falls so light,
A warmth ignites, despite the night.
Life contained in frozen streams,
Winter cradles all our dreams.

In stillness deep, the heart will race,
Finding beauty in winter's embrace.
A solace found, a spirit free,
In chilly breaths, we come to be.

Frigid Moments

In stillness deep, the shadows creep,
The world adorned in frosted dreams.
Each breath a cloud, so soft, so proud,
As winter whispers frozen themes.

Silent nights with silver light,
The stars reflect in icy streams.
Crisp air swirls, as joy unfurls,
In fleeting time, we share our beams.

Chill winds blow, as memories flow,
Each heartbeat echoes in the frost.
In every glance, there's a dance,
Where warmth and cold, together, tossed.

Hearts entwined in the pale moonshine,
As laughter twinkles, soft and clear.
We cherish these frigid embraces,
For moments spent, forever dear.

With every step, the world is kept,
In crystal magic, pure and bright.
Frigid moments, timeless echoes,
Embrace the night, hold on tight.

Timeless Glaciers

Majestic rise, the glaciers sigh,
A tapestry of ice and stone.
Ancient tales in silence pale,
They guard the world, forever known.

Like frozen waves, their beauty saves,
As sunlight glints on surfaces clear.
A dance of light in snowy white,
In timeless grace, they persevere.

Through ages past, so steadfast,
Their grandeur whispers to the air.
With every shift, they gently lift,
The secrets of a world so rare.

In icy crevices, time reminiscences,
Of nature's art, both fierce and grand.
The glaciers stand, a natural band,
In frozen realms, they proudly stand.

So let us gaze, through frosty haze,
At nature's wonders, vast and bold.
For in their might, we find the light,
Of stories yet to be retold.

A Dance in the Cold

Under the stars, where snowflakes fall,
We spin and sway, in winter's thrall.
Each twirl ignites the frosty air,
In whispered dreams, we dance with flair.

The chill embraces, hearts ignite,
As laughter sings in the pale moonlight.
Our footprints trace a path so bright,
A fleeting joy, a pure delight.

With arms entwined, we sway and glide,
In crystal hush, we seek to hide.
Through winter's night, our spirits soar,
In this cold embrace, we ask for more.

Each gust of wind becomes our friend,
As melodies of snow descend.
In every beat, our souls will blend,
A dance in the cold that will not end.

So hold me close, through night and frost,
In this fleeting moment, never lost.
Together we weave a tale so bold,
In the gentle art of a dance in the cold.

Melodies of the Frigid Air

Soft whispers float on winter's breath,
A song echoing through the chill.
Each note a touch, a moment much,
In melodies that time can't kill.

The pines sway gently, a choir in tune,
With every flake, a voice so sweet.
As frost unfolds, a story told,
In every heart, the rhythms beat.

Beyond the hills, the silence thrills,
A symphony of peace untold.
In frozen grace, we find our place,
In the orchestra of winter's hold.

As starlight weaves its silver lace,
Our spirits dance, in harmony sway.
With every breath, we feel the depth,
Of frigid air on this bright day.

So take a step, let magic prep,
For every sound that fills the night.
In winter's spell, we know so well,
The melodies of pure delight.

Chilling Embrace

In the stillness of night, a whisper calls,
Cold breezes dance through shadowed walls.
Embraced by frost, the world holds its breath,
A tranquil pause, a silence of death.

Snowflakes drift like dreams on a stream,
Softly caressing the heart's hidden seam.
Wrapped in white, the earth sighs deep,
In chilling embrace, all secrets sleep.

Branches bow down, heavy with grace,
Nature's cradle leaves no trace.
In this moment, time stands still,
A promise of warmth waits beyond the chill.

The horizon fades in a silver hue,
Stars blink softly, the night feels new.
Within this cold, a fire ignites,
Hope dances brightly, through freezing nights.

With every breath, the air bites sweet,
Yet love persists, through frostbitten heat.
Hold on tight, to warmth's sweet face,
In the heart of winter, find your place.

Glacial Thoughts

In icy realms where silence reigns,
Thoughts drift slow like winter's chains.
Chilled reflections in a frozen lake,
Whispers of dreams that silence makes.

Frozen peaks touch the azure sky,
Crisp air carries the soul's soft sigh.
Nature's canvas, stark yet bright,
Echoes of peace in the pale moonlight.

Fleeting moments in the chilly air,
Each thought a snowflake, uniquely rare.
Drifting slowly, lost in the haze,
Searching for warmth in the winter's gaze.

Through the cold, wisdom unfolds,
Stories of ages in silence told.
As glacial thoughts flow like streams of light,
Finding a pathway to warmth and flight.

In solitude's embrace, I wander free,
In frozen realms, I find the key.
To thaw the heart and let it soar,
In glacial thoughts, I explore more.

Fragments of a Frozen Dawn

Awake to whispers of a world anew,
Frozen dawn paints the heavens blue.
Gentle hues in the morning light,
Soft reminders that spring will fight.

Crystals glimmer on each blade of grass,
Nature's jewels, as moments pass.
The frost melts slowly, a hesitant sign,
That warmth and hope will soon entwine.

Birds awaken with gentle calls,
Fragments of dawn break down the walls.
A song of joy in the icy air,
Promises linger, a heart laid bare.

Each breath taken in the chilly morn,
Carries whispers of a world reborn.
In the fragments of light that shatter the night,
Hope finds its way, ever so bright.

Embrace the changes, let them unfold,
From fragments frozen, new stories told.
In the heart of dawn, where dreams take flight,
Find solace and strength in the gentle light.

Crystal Silence

In the depths of night, where shadows creep,
Crystal silence wraps the world in sleep.
Each breath is muffled, a secret kept,
In this stillness, the heart wept.

Light glimmers softly on snow-kissed ground,
Echoes of beauty in silence found.
Ancient trees stand guard, wise and tall,
Their branches cradle the night's sweet call.

Frozen moments like timeless art,
Crafted with patience, a work of heart.
Within the cold, love's warmth ignites,
In crystal silence, hope takes flight.

As stars wink softly in the velvet sky,
Thoughts float gently, like clouds drifting high.
Wrapped in stillness, the heart learns to dance,
In crystal silence, there's always a chance.

So hold this peace, let it surround,
In the lap of silence, let joy be found.
For in every moment, a whisper glows,
Telling stories that only the heart knows.

Whispering Glaciers

Ancient giants rise so still,
A breath of ice whispers through,
Dreams encased in frozen thrill,
Nature's secrets, old yet new.

Cracks and creaks in soft twilight,
Echoes of a world once warm,
Shadows dance in fading light,
A reminder of the storm.

Silent tales in every flake,
Drifting softly to the ground,
In their silence, dreams awake,
Magic wrapped in snowy sound.

Beneath their weight, the rivers sigh,
Yearning for a time to flow,
Yet beneath the endless sky,
They hold the tales of long ago.

Thawing Memories

Sunrise melts the frozen past,
Softly, slowly, thoughts return,
Moments captured, shadows cast,
In the warmth, the old hearts yearn.

Fingers glide on gentle streams,
Water whispers to the stone,
Revealing all our childhood dreams,
Where laughter once had freely grown.

Echoes of the playful days,
Buried deep in chilling cold,
Now they rise in misty haze,
Stories waiting to be told.

Each drop falls like a gentle tear,
Bringing life from what was lost,
In the thaw, we face our fear,
And reckon with the needed cost.

Glint of Frost

Underneath the morning light,
Glistening like stars on ground,
Frosty patterns, pure delight,
Nature's art in silence found.

Fragile crystals, sharp yet clear,
They reflect the world anew,
Each a story, bright and sheer,
A moment captured, frozen true.

Treading softly through the sheen,
Every step a careful dance,
In this world, serene, pristine,
Time and dreams hold quiet glance.

As the sun begins to rise,
Frost begins to slowly fade,
But the memories remain wise,
In the light, our hopes cascade.

Suspended in Freeze

Frozen still in silent pause,
Nature's breath hangs in the air,
Time stands still without a cause,
Every moment, just a prayer.

Branches bow with weight of frost,
Heavy-laden, bending low,
In this stillness, we are lost,
Searching for the strength to grow.

Hushed whispers in the crystal pale,
Remind us of the lives we led,
In this beauty, we exhale,
Finding peace in things unsaid.

As the world awaits the thaw,
Hope ignites a silent flame,
In the stillness, we withdraw,
Yet our hearts still hear their name.

Glacial Mornings

The dawn breaks cold and clear,
A blanket white laid near.
Chill whispers float through air,
Nature's breath, a frosty prayer.

Icicles hang like crystal swords,
Silence falls, no sound of words.
Sunrise paints the world in gold,
In this stillness, stories unfold.

Trees adorned in glistening sheen,
A landscape calm, serene, and clean.
Each step crunches, crisp and bright,
In the gentle morning light.

Birds call softly, wings in flight,
Over valleys pure and white.
The world wakes in icy grace,
Glacial morning's warm embrace.

With every breath, the frost does dance,
In this tranquil, frozen expanse.
Beauty found in frigid air,
Glacial mornings, rare, so fair.

Biting Shadows

Biting shadows creep and crawl,
Underneath the twilight's pall.
Whispers echo through the trees,
A chill that carries on the breeze.

Moonlight casts a silver glow,
Where we walk, and shadows grow.
Every corner holds a fright,
As the dark consumes the light.

Footsteps echo on the ground,
In the silence, fears abound.
Darkness wraps in cold embrace,
Haunting echoes, time and space.

Biting winds like ghostly sighs,
Startle dreams and pierce the skies.
Yet in the gloom, a spark may rise,
To light the path where courage lies.

In shadows deep, we find our way,
Braving night to greet the day.
Bound by fears, but hearts still bold,
Biting shadows, tales retold.

Whispered Frost

Whispered frost on midnight air,
Softly kisses, unaware.
Glittering upon the grass,
Nature's art, delicate as glass.

Silent moments breathe in peace,
In this hush, the world's release.
Time stands still, a frozen breath,
In the mystery of soft death.

Every flake tells a story true,
Of winter nights with skies so blue.
Stars like diamonds shimmer bright,
In the velvet cloak of night.

With each dawn, the colors blend,
Whispered frost textures ascend.
Life renewed in every freeze,
Melodies of nature tease.

So let us dance with moonlit dreams,
In whispered frost, the heart redeems.
Each gentle touch, a tale begun,
Whispered frost, a secret spun.

Timeless Freeze

In the stillness of the night,
Timeless freeze, pure and white.
Moments captured in the chill,
Nature's beauty, quiet thrill.

Clouds drift softly overhead,
A blanket of snow, bright and spread.
Each breath puffs like winter's sigh,
In this realm, the hours lie.

Frozen lakes mirror the skies,
Reflecting dreams and whispered lies.
Crystalline edges sparkle bright,
Ancient echoes, hearts ignites.

Footsteps trace the paths of yore,
In silent woods, a timeless lore.
Seasons change, yet here we stay,
In the freeze, we find our way.

As the stars twinkle soft and clear,
Whispers flow, we hold them dear.
In this solitude so grand,
Timeless freeze, forever planned.

Shiver of Time

Moments whisper, light as air,
Fleeting shadows, unaware.
Ticking clocks, they softly chime,
Every second, a shiver of time.

Memories dance on fragile wings,
Nostalgia's pull, it softly clings.
In the stillness, echoes rhyme,
Every heartbeat, a shiver of time.

Threads of fate in silken strands,
Weaving stories, dreams in hands.
Through the ages, mountains climb,
Every heartbeat, a shiver of time.

Youthful laughter, wisdom's grace,
In each line, a lingering trace.
As we stumble, as we mime,
Every heartbeat, a shiver of time.

In twilight's glow, we find our way,
Chasing light through dusk to day.
In the silence, memories prime,
Every heartbeat, a shiver of time.

Winter's Breath

Whispers rise with frosty air,
Winter's breath is everywhere.
Snowflakes dance with silent grace,
In their pause, a frozen face.

Branches bow with heavy snow,
Nature's quilt, a stunning show.
Under stars that gleam and shine,
Stillness wrapped in winter's spine.

Crimson berries 'gainst the white,
Cheery bursts in moon's soft light.
Shadows stretch as bluebirds sing,
Winter's breath, an echoing spring.

Footprints trace a secret path,
Laughter lingers in the aftermath.
Crackling fires with tales divine,
Moments cherished, all entwined.

As nights grow long and dreams take flight,
Embers glow, a cozy sight.
In this hush, our hearts align,
In the season's breath, we find.

Snowbound Reverie

Frosted windows, cozy glow,
Whispers of the winds that blow.
In the silence, dreams ignite,
Snowbound reverie, pure delight.

Every flake a world anew,
Lost in wonder, just we two.
Hot cocoa warms our hands so tight,
Snowbound reverie, cozy night.

Chasing shadows, laughter loud,
Draped in warmth beneath the cloud.
With each heartbeat, sparks take flight,
Snowbound reverie, pure delight.

Footsteps lead to hidden trails,
Stories told as twilight pales.
In each moment, dreams alight,
Snowbound reverie, hearts ignite.

As the evening gently fades,
Counting stars, our joy cascades.
We embrace the soft moonlight,
Snowbound reverie, pure delight.

Echoes of Frost

Morning breaks with icy gleam,
Nature whispers, sweet as dream.
Patterns etched on glassy pane,
Echoes of frost, winter's reign.

Breath clouds form in frosty air,
In the moment, silence rare.
Every branch, a crystal line,
Echoes of frost, pure design.

Chill descends with evening light,
Softly wrapping day to night.
Under stars the moon will shine,
Echoes of frost, nature's sign.

In the stillness, whispers play,
Ghostly forms in soft ballet.
Every sigh, a sacred rhyme,
Echoes of frost, bridge through time.

As we wander, hearts unfold,
Stories shared, both shy and bold.
In this magic, our souls align,
Echoes of frost, intertwined.

Surrendering to the Cold

Whispers of winter chill the air,
Frosted branches, a quiet dare.
The world is draped in white embrace,
Nature sleeps, a gentle pace.

Stars above in tranquil night,
Each twinkling jewel, a distant light.
Icicles hang like crystal dreams,
In this silence, nothing screams.

Shadows dance upon the ground,
With every step, a muffled sound.
Breath visible, mist in the night,
A tranquil world, wrapped up tight.

Snowflakes fall, a soft ballet,
Whirling softly, lost in play.
Footprints fade on frozen land,
A canvas crafted by unseen hand.

In this moment, time stands still,
The heart finds peace, a simple thrill.
Surrendering to the cold so deep,
In winter's lull, the world can sleep.

Snowfall's Lullaby

Listen close, the snowflakes sigh,
A gentle whisper, the winter's cry.
Blankets soft on earth's embrace,
Nature hums a sweetened grace.

Drifts of white in moonlit glow,
A peaceful world, wrapped in snow.
Dreams aloft in hazy flight,
Cradled softly by the night.

Children's laughter fills the air,
Snowmen stand with frosty flair.
Each flake a tale, each drift a song,
In this beauty, we all belong.

As night unfolds its silken shawl,
Snowfall's lyrics begin to call.
To all who wander, hearts set free,
Embrace the magic, let it be.

In the hush, a secret sound,
Of winter's heart, so pure, profound.
Swaying gently, dreams comply,
To the rhythm of snowfall's lullaby.

Echoes in the Glaze

The world is trapped in crystal light,
Silhouettes blurred, a ghostly sight.
Footsteps crunch on icy ground,
Echoes whisper all around.

Trees adorned in shimmering coats,
Nature's art, as winter gloats.
Every branch a story told,
In the silent, biting cold.

Frozen lakes, a glassy sheen,
Reflections of what might have been.
The breeze carries secrets old,
In the glaze, memories unfold.

Winds weave through the frozen air,
Each breath a promise, a fleeting prayer.
Living echoes, soft yet clear,
In this frost, the past draws near.

Twilight settles, the day must fade,
In winter's hold, the dreams cascade.
Listen close, to the night's gentle phase,
In the silence, echoes blaze.

Slumber Beyond the Frost

Beneath the frost, the earth lies still,
A waiting pulse, a quiet thrill.
In winter's cloak, life holds its breath,
While dreams of spring lie deep beneath.

Snowflakes fall, a frozen veil,
Covering secrets in tranquil pale.
Roots intertwined in the shaded ground,
Whisper of life without a sound.

Nature's pause, a whispered peace,
From the world, a gentle release.
Time marches on in a frosty haze,
But underneath, the heart still plays.

Icicles hang like jeweled art,
Guardians of dreams, waiting to start.
In slumber's grip, the warmth will rise,
Beyond the frost, the sun will prize.

Patient blooms, with hope enshrined,
Await the call of springtime's wind.
For now, let the silence host,
Our slumber waiting, beyond the frost.

Milton Keynes UK
Ingram Content Group UK Ltd.
UKHW010230111224
452348UK00011B/648